Contents

1. Getting Started – The Kickoff 3

2. Writing Requirements 7

3. Designing Your Solution 12

4. The Clickable Demo 16

5. Milestones and Project Plans 19

6. Testing and Verification 22

7. Securing Your Solution 25

8. Add The Finishing Touches 28

9. Declaring Victory – Ship It! 31

Creating Software – Turning
Your Vision Into An Application

Getting Started – The Kickoff

The first step in a project is the kickoff. This may be a meeting of your team or just a time for you to commit your vision to paper. The primary step in a kickoff is to clearly define your "why." Knowing the reason why you are building an application is critical on your journey. The "why" of your project helps you define where you are going and parameters for the trip. Do not stop with just defining it either. The team should have the "why" communicated to them, and that should provide a focus during design, implementation, and beyond. The better the "why" is defined and understood by the team, the less likely there will be functional or other drift.

What Problem Are We Solving?

Once we capture why we are building the application, the next step is to be clear on the problem we are solving. This does not have to be a complex process. First, we define our project at a high level. Next, we list the problem or problems we are solving. The problem solved is the answer to an important question, "Why should anyone care?" If you struggle to define the problem being solved the product will likely fail.

We do not start projects just to spin our wheels. There is always a problem that is being solved, and that is what gives the project value.

It is also important for us to keep our target audience in mind as we implement our vision. However, it is arguably more important to keep the problem we aim to solve at the forefront. The audience will disappear if you do not provide value.

What Are Our Assumptions?

This question is a tough one. Unfortunately, it is where a lot of the pitfalls live. When a project is envisioned, there are often factors that we take for granted. For example, let's consider building an application that makes it easy to move money among bank accounts.

The Steps For Starting Your Project

• Clearly Define the "Why"

• Describe the problem(s) you are solving with the application

• What are The Business Goals? (constraints around your solution)

• Identify the key stakeholders and subject matter experts

• Create The Budget (Time and Money)

• Who is the target Audience?

• What are the risks?

• Define the Requirements or Feature List

• Create a list of key milestones, features, and deliverables

The key in these steps is to spend time clearly defining the project early on where the cost of changes are negligible. This early focus on design will greatly improve our chances for success.

We can assume that there is a login, user authentication, bank account linking features, error messages, fraud restrictions, and much more. All of these functions are critical to the success of the project, but easily overlooked when we ask a team to implement it. Make your assumptions clear from the start.

What Can Go Wrong?

A lot of software projects fall short of expectations. This takes the form of budget overruns, slipped schedules, or broken functionality. Unfortunately, there are enough projects that fall into this category that we need to do some defensive planning and reduce our risk of failure.

This is a step where two things are assessed and listed. There are the risks to the project success. The risks include lack of resources, lack of funding, competition beating us to market, etc. The second item is the exceptions within the solution. These include handling bad data, loss of needed connectivity, and even things like a forgotten password.

At this point, none of these items need to be addressed at a detailed level; they just need to be considered.

The goal at this time is to ensure that we are aware of potential risks and pitfalls. Then we can plan to address or mitigate them. We also might find priorities that come out of this action. For example, the market window for a product may be known to close in a certain time frame. The product has to be completed in that period to have any chance of success. Thus, meeting our schedule is critical to success (very high priority). For more information check out this Gartner Article

The key to any successful project is to have a sound reason why the user will find value in the result. Consider this reason as the spirit of the solution. There is more value when the application is not just a solution that is technically correct, it is also useful. A common disconnect of users and designers is that the solution is not the focus.

This is not unlike a bill in Congress that starts out simple like "make X illegal" and ends up a thousand pages of riders and side projects that have nothing to do with the original goal. When a project starts with well-defined goals that persist as the core requirements, then success is more likely.

Scope creep is an often underestimated phrase. The actual result is closer to an avalanche. Each little variation from the core goals of the project can spawn other variations. It is not uncommon to lose weeks of project implementation focused on features that were initially ignored. It is important to define what a solution will not be. However, the key to success is making sure that those "not in" features do not creep in later.

Make Your Hard Work Pay Off

- **Do not stop with a definition**. Make the why of the project known to all the players.

- **Keep it front and center**. Schedule regular reviews of the requirements and plans to ensure that the why persists throughout the life of the project. Use it as your cornerstone for any feature decisions.

- **Your project cornerstone.** Builders use a cornerstone to keep their buildings on track and properly aligned. Use the "why" of your project for the same.

- **Back To Basics**. When in doubt, you should always be able to tie a decision back to the why that started it all.

Why Worry About Why?

One of the biggest weaknesses I experience when consulting on projects is a lack of why. When the champion of the project is asked about the purpose of the project, there is an answer. However, the answer is about a vision, not about solving a problem. Solving a problem is critical and there should be a reason why that problem needs to be solved. Otherwise, we may create a solution in search of a problem.

An ill-defined solution can be an issue for a project. This is because a cool idea is not the same as people needing a fresh idea to solve their problems.

We have all seen this situation with products that have a lot of fanfare but then fall flat on their face. For those that remember the dot-com boom of the late nineties, there are several companies that fit this mold. The site Pets.com went nowhere. There were also a whole series of groceries on demand websites that never got beyond a memorable mascot or name.

The struggle with your "why" and the problem you are solving is to keep them both in mind. This is a critical part of creating a successful product. When you blend these two attributes you end up with a solution that has a reason. That means you get a solution that people will use instead of just a solution. For example, an abacus can solve the problem of making addition easier. However, a calculator keeps in mind the "why" of being able to easily solve the same problems. Both are solutions, one has a more attractive "why."

Think it through.

The easiest way to test our idea is to toss out a solution and then have the team discuss its viability. You will find this approach works best when it includes stakeholders and end users in some fashion. Design by committee is not something I recommend.

However, I do find that examining a solution in an open forum is highly likely to point out the flaws. When you find the why of a project, follow up with an examination of alternatives. This provides a way to verify why THIS solution and to increase your odds of success.

The Bottom Line

Before you move on from the kick-off, make sure you have your ducks in a row. You would be foolish to start a road trip without making sure you have your bags packed and a destination set. There is no difference in starting a software project. Be sure of where you want to end up. That alone will help reduce the risk in reaching your destination.

Writing Requirements

There is a discernable difference between novice and veteran requirement writers. Part of this difference is due to the process being more art than science. However, it still has some best practices that can be of help to anyone. In this chapter, we will explore some points to consider that can help make your next requirements document the best one you have written yet.

That being said, every time you write requirements there should be an improvement over prior attempts. I have not found any perfect requirement documents in my experience. That means we can always make improvements. Also noteworthy is that perfection is not our goal, that can lead to analysis paralysis, focus on completeness instead.

Start With An Outline

In my experience, this is the most natural step. Start with a high-level overview of needs for the project. The overview helps set the stage for greater detail while providing a core design. It is important to have this basic design as it provides a reference point as the details are refined which can help avoid drift.

Once the outline is created it can, and should, be regularly referenced during the definition of detailed requirements to ensure the details link back to core features.

The highest level outline of requirements is the vision for the project. This outline is the general view of what is to be created. The sub-sections of the outline are used to drive tighter definition of features and expectations.

Then Build on That Outline

Once the outline comes together, it is time to go to the next level. This is the point where most requirements fall apart. However, there are a set of questions that a well-defined requirement will answer. Let's look at each question and what to consider in answering it.

Six Questions Our Requirements Should Answer

How do I get to this point? This question looks at how a requirement is executed. It includes considering who can access a feature. Then examine whether there are limits for different users or times. For example, one requirement of an ATM is to dispense money. To receive cash, someone must be authenticated to the system (card and PIN). Then the authenticated user must make a request for withdrawal. Also, the account must be selected, and it has to have a balance greater than the sum to dispense. Keep this example in mind as we look at the other questions.

**"Show the new guy here around.
Clue him in on our ridiculous expectations."**

What is the expectation when this requirement is fulfilled? At this point, we define what is needed for the requirement to be met. If we can not determine success or failure of a requirement, then it is either not needed or ill-defined. For example, an ATM withdrawal will result in cash dispensed to the user and the account debited. There may be new expectations as well, but they should all be defined as part of answering this question.

What happens if an error occurs? This is the question most often missed in my experience. A well-defined vision is all about the success of the system, but errors occur. The way those errors are handled must be defined as well. In the ATM example, a user might not have a high enough balance in their account. Likewise, the machine might not have enough cash on hand. Other errors can occur as well. The list of potential errors can get lengthy, but they need to be examined and documented.

What data should I have once I get to this requirement? This is a how we address the state or environment we can expect in meeting a need. It potentially includes defining how the data is gathered and disseminated. Thus, we might find requirements that will need to be determined while answering this question. In the above ATM example, we should have an account number, an authenticated flag and an amount to withdraw. Therefore, we will have requirements defined that address how an account number is gathered, how to authenticate a user, and how to tell the system what to withdraw.

Design Drift

Drift from the outline and vision is highly discouraged. It does not mean the vision cannot be altered or refined. However, a project is a plan for moving from A to B. The B is the vision. Therefore, changing B as the focus can create situations where you "take the scenic route" or even become hopelessly lost.

Where do I go from this requirement? The first question we asked was the entry into a requirement. This question tells us how we exit. Once a requirement is fulfilled, we need to examine the options for proceeding. Often the answer to this issue is a list of "locations" based on success or failure. In the ATM example, we can show a success message, an error screen, or might go back to the main menu. During this step we might turn up some other entry requirements to define. For example, is there a "quick cash" option that skips going back to the main menu and instead logs the user out after dispensing cash?

What happens if an error occurs? This is the question most often missed in my experience. A well-defined vision is all about the success of the system, but errors occur. The way those errors are handled must be defined as well. In the ATM example, a user might not have a high enough balance in their account. Likewise, the machine might not have enough cash on hand. Other errors can occur as well. The list of potential errors can get lengthy, but they need to be examined and documented.

Do I need to communicate success or failure of this requirement? This question is skipped more often than not in my experience. Once a requirement can be considered a success or failure, we must determine if a notification needs to occur? This may be a report, a log entry, or any other communication method. We might even want to provide multiple responses. In the ATM example, the notification is likely a printed receipt (report), a beep or sound to note the process is complete, and a message on the screen.

Creating User Stories

This is an excellent exercise to help build out your requirements. It is a practice that helps us keep in mind the why, how, and the "what else?" of any requirement or feature. To be clear, the goal of a user story is to focus on the problem being solved and the experience of that solution for the user. Nevertheless, the details of the story should all be addressed within a requirements document. In some cases, the user stories can provide you the top level items of the requirements outline.

The practice of user stories also serves a purpose of linking your technical and business users to an explanation they all can understand and agree on. Thus, it is an excellent way to test workflows, avoid miscommunication and clarify translation errors among the groups. They provide an excellent way to discuss your solution before you start implementing it.

The Key Parts of a User Story

- **A general description or summary** and possibly an ID value to make it easy to point to exactly which user story is being viewed.

- **A "happy path"** or story that works correctly and meets all expectations.

- **Exceptions** that highlight what can go wrong. We do not need to implement how these are handled, just note that they can exist. (see also assumptions below)

- **Assumptions** that we make to get to the happy path. These provide us a staring point for the story and might point to other stories that have been created.

- **Priority, frequency, or some other weight** to convey the importance of this story in the system being created.

Your specific needs for each story will vary. Thus, consider these parts as rough suggestions rather than tightly defined bullet points. An example follows to help you build out your own custom templates for building a user story. Feel free to take this as a first step and edit it to serve your purposes.

An Example User Story

ID:	PC-1
Title:	Create a Product
Description:	A User wants to add a product to the system without resorting to an import from files.
Primary Actor:	General Staff
Preconditions:	User is logged into System (see story AU-1)
Postconditions:	New Product is available to edit/publish
Main Success Scenario:	1. User creates a product by clicking new product option or by duplicating an existing one 2. User populates/updates product properties 3. Default values are set where applicable 4. Product defaults to not live so it is not automatically published 5. Product is saved and available for further editing 6. Data is pushed to the production site to configure product in that system
Extensions:	1. For this use case a Product may also be a SKU 2. Product id plus SKU plus supplier must be unique 3. Manufacturer part number is unique id for a product (but may have multiple suppliers) 4. User will be notified of failure to save product due to validation or system issues 5. All attributes are available on initial creation (see appendix for list) 6. Note that this implies the product can be added quickly and without entering values for all fields.
Frequency of Use:	Frequent
Status:	Pending Review
Owner:	Product Management
Priority:	Critical

Designing Your Solution

The most critical part of a successful software project is getting the design right. All of us have a tendency to think that implementation can correct a weak design. That leads us to assume this step is not the most important. Of course, there is also a tendency towards low success rates in software projects. Maybe those two are related?

Think about constructing a house. If the architect creates a blueprint that is incorrect or fuzzy then how well do you think that will work out? A challenge with proper design is that it takes relevant experience to get it right. You can read volumes about designing software. Unfortunately, we have found that experience is the best teacher and every project has its own special circumstances.

We Have Taken Some Excellent First Steps

One of the ways to improve the odds of a good design is to start with good requirements. In fact, bad requirements will inevitably lead to bad design. Gaps in our requirements can not only lead to gaps in design, they can lead to a need for re-work on implementation. All of this can be tracked back to incorrect design. That means the previous steps we discussed of requirements creation and user stories is a critical part of creating software successfully. Once we have the requirements completed, it is time to turn those into a design. We will find a lot of similarities in these early steps.

Requirements are a Checklist for Design

While the stories give us an outline, the requirements tell us the details we must include in our design. I have seen requirements and specifications documents often used exactly as a checklist. The designer literally walks through those documents and checks off sections, sentences, and even words to make sure those have been addressed in the design. When you think of it that way, it shows how important the details of the requirements document are.

Helpful Hint: Stories Translate to Screens and Roles

The User stories provide us with a form of checklist for user roles, application pages or forms, and key interactions. Use these to build an outline for the design to help avoid gaps. A design that does not completely address all of the user stories is incomplete by definition. Therefore, we should start by using those stories to tell us the pieces of a complete design.

Six Properties of a Thorough Design

Create a Complete Interface. This may appear to be stating the obvious, but there are a lot of details that are easy to overlook. The main screens and pages of the application will jump out at us. However, a good design includes things like messages, notifications, reports, and even emails. This last item is becoming more common as users look for communication from applications outside of actually running the application. Thus, we need to design not only when emails and notifications are sent, but how they look and the information they contain.

Include all of the roles and masking for each. There are almost always multiple types of users that we need to address in the design. These roles need to be thoroughly addressed in the design. Common gaps in roles are: how they are administered, what they can access, how they interact with data, and how the application flows differ for each. When in doubt, go back to your user stories to ensure that you have defined the roles that are needed to support them.

Define the exceptions and error handling. It may come as a surprise but applications have errors and exceptions. A good design will plan for these and provide ways to recover from them. Avoid designing for only the "happy path." Make sure you include the assumptions and expectations along with how the system should react when those are not met. This is another key factor in being able to test the solution. The testers need to know what to expect when they break the application.

Include the infrastructure and foundation with the design. There is more to an application than meets the eye. Include the non-visual pieces in your design as well. Modern applications require a sound infrastructure including security, logging, audit trails, and other items that a user will likely never see. This step is also where the user view of the application (requirements) gets translated into implementation details. A User Story describes features and responses that imply things to the technical team. For example, a requirement for multiple user roles implies permissions and authentication is supported by the system. A good designer reads between the lines of the requirements to create a complete system.

Define the data to be tracked and how it will flow. It is easy to forget data even though it is the lifeblood of an application. A good design has to include not only what must be captured, but also where it will be stored and how to retrieve it. Validation is often an area where the design is limited.

Ensure that the design provides the constraints on data that are expected or necessary. One other area where designs tend to be lacking is the disposal of data. Do not forget to design how data is to be deleted or disabled and include details about archiving of data if that is needed.

Provide expectations and guidelines for testing. A good requirements document provides an excellent outline for testing but the design should take it to a more detailed level. The screens, data, validations, outputs, and reporting should leave nothing to be guessed by the testing team. In fact, when the testing team uses the design as a source for building their scripts, the process serves as an excellent way to test the completeness of the design.

An Example Design

Name:	User Home Page
Navigation/How To Get Here:	On Login or Select Home Page menu option from top level menu of any screen.
Description:	This is the primary page to drive user information and navigation. They will start using the application from this screen no matter what role or permissions they have.
User Restrictions:	None, All users can go to this screen.
Sections/Features:	• Welcome message and current account status • Logout link • Current task list • Recent activity history list • System and user account messages
Data used:	• User Profile • User Tasks • System Messages • User Messages • User history
Data Modified:	• None
Actions Allowed:	• View Tasks • View Messages • Create New Task • View/Edit Profile
Assumptions/Validations:	• User must be logged in • Account must be active
Exceptions:	• Send user to login screen if not logged in • Send user to profile management page if the account is not active
Special Considerations:	• Display "Nothing for you to do" if the task list is empty • Display "No Entries Found" if the history list is empty • Hide the message section if there is no system or user message • User messages have a green background • System messages have a red background
Data Requirements:	• Current Task: Start date, Due date, status, title, sort by due date ascending • Activity history: Action name, timestamp of activity, sort by date descending • Messages: Creation date of message, Title, Source of Message, message type, first 100 characters of the message, link to view full message
Notes:	This page follows the common page format with a header, footer, navigation menu and content displayed in the content section. See the page template design for more information. When an action does not have an obvious return location then send the user to this page. This includes any save and close functions performed throughout the application.

The template above is provided to give you some suggestions for designing screens. There is no screen mockup or wireframe provided. However, it is highly recommended that you include these, where possible, to assist in the implementation. There should also be a section of your design that covers all of the data requirements (name, type, size, etc.) in detail. Many of those details will be found spread across screens. Nevertheless, a central location to see the data types, relations, and constraints will make reading and understanding your design easier.

The Clickable Demo

One of the challenges with any project is getting everyone on the same page. Over the years, I have found that the best tool to help solve this problem is a clickable demo. This demo is so useful it is often one of the first steps in a new project. Creating the clickable demo can be simple and straightforward or a big effort in itself. However, these actions make even a complex system easier to model and discuss.

An important part of the clickable demo is an example of the application flow. When use cases are properly done, they should be a stepping stone to the application flow. The use cases will not provide all of the details, but a good demo will address every user story. Note that the look and feel of the demo are not as important initially as the flow. It should model how a user will progress through the application while providing a rough approximation of the data they will be presented. General navigation should be worked in early on as well. The full user experience can evolve in later iterations.

SOFTWARE DEMO

Leave Room For Discussion

The purpose of this demo-based approach is to provide a focal point for customers. Don't be afraid to leave a few areas open to interpretation. Also, avoid getting designed into a corner. The demo is not necessarily production code, so spending a lot of time on it may be a wasted effort. As iterations of the demo are presented there will be areas that become concrete. Early on try to avoid lock-in where possible.

Some requirements are more important than others. The requirements that a good clickable demo presents will include those around data input and output as well as reporting. Thus, When a customer is reviewing a clickable demo, they should be able to tie the navigation steps into currently defined use cases. This link is best accomplished by showing details around each step. Then the demo becomes a novel that combines the user stories.

For example, let's consider an application that includes data entry and search for entered records. A good clickable demo will show the input fields as close as possible to the end product. Size and amount will help even if the data is not "real." The search, in this case, should allow a search on enough of the data entry fields to be easy to find any given record. With these pieces in place, a customer should be given a good feel of how difficult or easy the interface will be for regular usage.

A clickable demo is a living and evolving step in the process of building your application. The demo can be added to and improved in a series of iterations with a review at each step along the way. Done this way, each demo should be an improvement no the prior ones.

The best use of it is to keep coming back for reviews and discussions. It can be a way to provide checkpoints throughout your project to confirm that it is on track according to the customer as well as the designers.

Risks Of A Clickable Demo

I started with a claim of this approach being perfect for any project. That does not mean it is not without risks. The most common issue with a demo of this type is that it is "too good." In that situation, a customer falls in love with the demo. The result is not a criticism, but instead something along the lines of "when can we ship it?" This tricky situation can be avoided by clearly stating what is smoke and mirrors. Also mention the mocked up functionality during the walkthrough. Obviously fake data helps too.

Set the expectations early, and clearly. This will avoid confusion or a masking of the effort required to make the demo fully functional. Avoid implying too much simplicity in your solution.

The problem with a vision is that it is not reality. Thus, everyone is left to their interpretation of the goals. Try a clickable demo next time to turn a vision into reality early in a project life-cycle. The effort will make discussions of the vision much easier and will help avoid a misunderstanding of conceptual features.

Key Features to Include In Your Demo

- **General navigation** items like menus and buttons. Use placeholders pages when helpful.

- The header, footer, and **general look-and-feel** parts of the application. Work towards a demo that encapsulates the user experience.

- The **key features and highest priority requirements** that have a visual component. This will be shown to stake-holders so it is a visual model by nature.

- Features and functions that have a **high risk** of getting done or difficult problems that need to be solved.   A good demo also provides a proof-of-concept for critical challenges of the solution.

- **Examples** of reports, notifications, and messages

- A **flow** that matches the highest priority user stories.

- Any **concerns** or hot-button issues for your customers. Make sure they see (at least) the features they expect to see or require in a complete solution.

Milestones and Project Plans

No one starts a journey without thinking about how to get to the destination. Steps in a random direction may take us in the opposite direction of our goal. Software projects are the same as any other journey. We need to plan our approach for implementation. Just like a higher definition map helps us better plot a journey, a well-defined project plan improves our odds for success in building software.

One of the important parts of planning and tracking project progress is defining milestones. These are points during the project where required tasks and goals for time meet, we can also call these checkpoints. Thus. it only makes sense that the definition of milestones and how they are treated are an important part of a sound plan.

We have a design and solid ideas about how this should work. Therefore, it is now time to look into building out a project plan. As we have in the other areas, we start at a high level with milestones and then drill down to get a detailed plan.

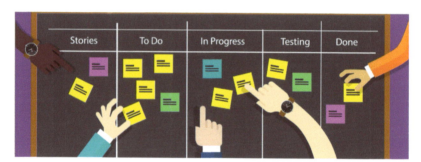

Steps for Building Good Milestones

Before we dive into defining milestones, there are a few items to note. Although these steps in the definition process are necessary, that does not mean they have to be complex. Every project is different, but I have found the guidelines below to be useful. In fact, I use them every time we need to craft milestones. Every milestone should have these properties, but they can be assumed rather than something that must be formally declared or documented. For example, a milestone of a design document can be all you need to list and still cover all of these properties. There is no need to go into deep detail about what that document contains or its structure.

Milestones must have a deliverable. Defining the deliverable for a milestone is rarely a problem. However, I have seen vague descriptions like "complete the application UI" as the total of the objective. This description is a start, but not truly definable. Nor is there a deliverable mentioned. We have to be able to say a milestone is complete (or not) without ambiguity. The example above is improved by including a UI demo to be delivered as part of the objective.

Provide a Method For Feedback. Milestones are more than just getting work done. They are also an opportunity to gather customer feedback. Use the milestone deliverables as a way to verify the implementation is still on track with the vision and goals of the client. This option helps deliver a successful solution instead of just delivering a project.

The deliverable must be visible to the customer. This point is often an issue during a project. There will be a step that includes securing the site or building a backend database. Unfortunately, the implementation does not have a visible result. That is not okay. Find a way to craft the deliverable so that the customer can see that progress has been made. The progress may be a login screen tied to an ACL or the result of some select statements to show default data in a database. When in doubt, modify the milestones, so the "invisible" work is part of visible steps.

Avoid Defining Milestones in a Vacuum.

The full team is not always a part of the project definition. Thus, we run into projects that are ill-defined and yet, we still want them to be successful. In these cases, I find it is best to break the work you control (or are assigned) into milestones. Your position in the team may not allow for customer feedback as part of milestone delivery. However, you can usually find someone to which the deliverable can be presented. Every little bit helps.

Defining Milestones For Success

We have already alluded to milestones being about more than progress. They can also be designed to improve the chances of a successful project. As mentioned earlier, the first step is to ensure that customer feedback is part of delivering any milestone. This goal can be achieved through regular demos and review sessions that coincide with milestone deliverables or as simple as a feedback email.

I find that presenting milestone deliverables in some way is useful for drawing out feedback as well as a sort of test of the deliverables. This not only helps the customer relate to the application and demo, it also provides a story board for your presentation. That extra review of the deliverable can be a sanity check while also revealing gaps.

Scheduling the milestones in a way to reduce risk is recommended. When the milestones that have the most risk are tackled early in a project, the schedule can be more solid and reliable sooner rather than later. Of course, that is not always possible. In most cases, the work on challenging items early in a project is a way to bring up estimation issues and slippage with enough time to make adjustments, if needed.

Testing And Verification

I do not want to shock you, but software often has bugs. We may call these "features" or "known issues" but in the end they are bugs. These defects are just part of being human and trying to craft large and complex solutions. Sometimes we make mistakes. The challenge with these errors is finding and eradicating them whenever possible. Thus, improving quality. That is where testing comes in.

It is important to note that testing comes in many shapes and sizes. There are unit tests for early in implementation through to system and acceptance tests on the back end of the implementation phase. All of these combine to help us feel comfortable with the value of the solution we deliver. So let's look at some good testing approaches to include in our project.

Common Testing Types

There are a dozen or more types of testing I have run into over the years. Thankfully, we do not need all of them for every solution. Instead, we will focus on testing types that should be utilized for every project based on their focus. It is worth mentioning that the listed test types are for typical releases and do not include maintenance and update tests like regression and chaos that are equally valuable once our solution has been "shipped." These are a critical factor in delivering a product that your customers can rely on and does not flood your team with support calls.

Note: We are focusing on testing approaches and strategies in this chapter. However, there are phases like Alpha and Beta versions that can provide great value for testing and validation. We do not want to ship overly buggy versions during these periods as the focus at that point should be on acceptance and user feedback rather than functional testing of our code.

Testing Type Definitions

Type	Definition
Unit	Validation of a small piece of code or functionality. The tested item should stand on its own with minimal (preferably none) side effects.
Integration	Validating that units work together properly
System	The next step from integration and validates the system as a whole works. This tests design and requirements as well as the implementation
Smoke	Short and Easy to run tests for a deployment to validate that the code was properly deployed
User Acceptance (UAT)	Validation that the users/customers want what is being delivered. This is focused primarily on meeting the requirements (explicit and implicit).

Common Approaches To Testing

Start simple and test the happy path. Happy path testing is the approach most developers take. The data entered and options selected exactly follow expected usage patterns. This sort of testing does not trigger any validation issues and all data is safely within any of the constraints. For example, an ATM withdrawal happy path would include the PIN is entered correctly the first time, the account is valid, the amount to withdraw is available for the balance and the cash is on hand for the machine. This type of testing should almost always succeed without issue.

Cover every possible exception in your testing. This is effectively the opposite of happy path testing. We talked about exceptions and potential errors in the design and requirements. The tests should verify that these behave as expected.

We hope our users follow the happy path, but we can expect they will encounter exceptions and errors. Part of this process is to consider the possible problems before we start implementation. That provides the best sort of testing and verification. We should not be surprised by how our users access (and break) the solution.

Null, empty, and missing values should be tested wherever applicable. It is easy to enter random data in fields as part of our testing. On the other hand, we can easily forget to leave fields blank. Our validations should handle a lot of this sort of testing, but nearly every application has situations where users can enter no data. Make sure the entry through to output and reporting is tested for empty values.

Make sure you test all constraints, min, max, exact and one off. A lot of errors show up in the "off by one" areas. Make sure you test just above, just below, and exact values at the top and bottom of constraints. For example if your valid values are 1 – 10 then your testing should include 0,1,2,9,10, and 11. It is not uncommon to shortcut some of these values. However, when you cover them all it will substantially reduce the bugs that turn up later.

Deployment environments and testing impacts. One of the best practices related to testing is to maintain multiple environments. Typically, these are development, QA/Test, and production at least. There are occasionally UAT, training and sales environments as well. These environments are critical to the team's ability to execute tests and provide good feedback when errors occur. Even small teams of a couple of developers will find their testing to be smoother and more effective with the "big 3" environments of Dev, Test, and Prod.

Test variations that are to be supported. Browser testing has become much more common than it was in the past. However, this form of testing is easily overlooked. It is almost impossible to build a web application for only one browser type in this day and time so make sure you cover the popular and recent browsers in the market.

In a similar vein, test things like languages, time zones, currencies, and both connected and disconnected variations. These should be thoroughly tested, if you support them. All of these variables that come from varying user environments can cause huge issues if you forget to test them.

Finally, test usage on minimum machine configurations when applicable. This should include small memory, small screens, and minimal disk storage space.

Securing Your Solution

Security is a hot topic among the IT world. When we build an application we will be asked about the measures we have taken to secure the data and protect users. This means we need to make sure we have followed best practices in our design, implementation, and delivery. Let's look at what steps we should take to provide comfort to ourselves and our customers.

Everyone is a Target

Our customers want assurances that their data will be safe in our solution. However, that is just one reason why security is something that we need to build into our applications. We never know when we will be a target of an attack. Although we can not guarantee the failure of attack attempts, we can at least take steps to reduce the chances of success and make it easier to acknowledge breaches to our customers.

Expectations of Security

When you create an application it is expected to be secure. That is just what customers want from a professional solution. This is the case whether it is on-premise/installed or a cloud solution. Thus, you do not want to wait until product launch to find out what steps should have been taken to comfort the customers. Every type of application is at least a little different in what is expected and what needs to be secured. That is the first step at this point. We need to assess where our potential security risks are, the industry standards for addressing them and any applicable compliance requirements.

The best approach is to hire a security professional to assess and audit your solution. However, that can cost thousands of dollars and take weeks to complete. We can take some steps that will provide much of that security at a fraction of the cost.

The suggestions below are easy to implement. Therefore, they should be considered before deploying or shipping any application whether for internal or external use. These will help with your overall assessment during a security audit, but should be considered first steps. The compliance, reliability, and security of your application are key factors in its success. Thus, you should take additional steps as best practices suggest to provide the level of security your customers expect.

Security Steps You Should Always Take

Limit the number of points of entry. Whether you want to secure an application, a device, or a network, the first step for security is limiting the options for entry. This is often accomplished through a firewall when the focus is a device or network. Limit the ways that outsiders can get into the system. That simple step makes it easier to guard those access points. The more holes you have, the harder it is to block all of those points of entry.

With an application, you can do this through limiting the ways to login or run the application. Even better, create multiple versions of the application where functionality is not even available on versions targeted at specific users. This is not common in modern software. However, it would not be hard to design a user and administrator version of the application where the administrator functionality code does not even exist in the user version.

Limit feedback information to a need to know basis. The User Experience is an important part of any application. The challenge is that simplifying access to the system is often in direct conflict with security. The easier it is for a user to access the system, the easier it is for hackers to do the same.

This often becomes an issue when the notifications are being crafted. In particular, the ones that deal with failed logins. A user will be able to fix a failed login more easily when they know that they got the user id correct, but the password wrong. Of course that is assuming that the user id they entered is the one they wanted to use. In any case, when we let the user know that the login entered is valid, but not the password, we provide a hacker with half the information they need to access the system. Generic notifications like "Login Failed" are not very helpful to our users. On the other hand, they are not very helpful to hackers either. Consider that whether crafting a message or designing an informative UI. Too much information can be a security risk

Clean up the developer messages and shortcuts. This is one of those steps you should take even when security is not a concern. We have all been known to take a shortcut with a message during development or to plug in some code to help with debugging. This can be an annoyance (or even insulting) to a user. Likewise, it can be a key to cracking security for a hacker. Do a pass through the code and application to note any places where some cleanup is required.

Protect the secret sauce. Every technology has its strengths and weaknesses. This includes the area of security. There are back doors and weak areas of an application based on what is used to build it. That includes the version as well as the broader technology. We all like to brag on our technology and how it helps us create a better solution. That is a habit we need to overcome.

There is rarely a business need for divulging our technology or architecture. Even when there is, we can often stay a bit vague to thwart hackers. If you find that not to be the case then at least have customers sign a non-disclosure agreement to help keep the details from showing up in the public domain. The less information about our application available to hackers, the more they have to learn to break into our system.

Password security through strength and limited availability. When you start looking closely at why system security is breached there are a few reasons that always show up at the top. One of these is password security or strength. The most common password is "password123" and it is used a scary amount of the time. Make your passwords impossible to guess, lengthy, and mix in special characters where possible. As you are able, make your users do the same. This can be an inconvenience. However, the security it brings is worth the tradeoff.

Follow Best Practices. There are countless security articles and posts available that apply to your situation. Stay current on these new bits of contents and suggestions for keeping your data secure. You need to be careful of the source of these articles but otherwise they are a perfect source for best practices and smart steps to secure your environment. Do a final review before you deploy for release.

Add The finishing Touches

If you have ever watched a cooking competition like Master Chef or admired a meal from a four-star cook then you have experienced finishing touches. The product is more than just food in these cases. The presentation, nuances, and subtle combination of tastes make the meal a work of art. A software product is very similar. You can craft source code and produce an application that solves an important problem while still failing commercially.

Commercial software is as much about how you solve the problem and the user experience as the raw solution itself. That is why the little editor program you build as a class project is not even close to a competitor to Microsoft Word. The features contribute to the difference in an application and product, but only partially. There are a number of finishing touches we need to perform before our product becomes a commercial application.

Expectations For Commercial Applications are High
There are many expectations customers have for a commercial application. These often unspoken requirements are easy to overlook. However, that does not reduce their importance. It is critical to review the finishing touches we need to make before we can declare that our application ready for release.

First Impressions Are Vital

We have probably all experienced the situation where we are excited about a purchase only to be disappointed when we get it. This may be something we unwrap that dashes our hopes or something delivered that is far below expectations. With software products, this may be immediately apparent, or our dismay can come after days of using the product.

Oops Can Be Crippling

We all recognize that mistakes happen. Sometimes a bad first impression can be overcome. Unfortunately, we do not always know a bad impression has been made. Think of being served what is to you obviously spoiled food at a restaurant. Will you call the manager or just get up and leave? Software is easy to ignore and talk bad about. If you want to be successful then you want to pay off the trust a customer has given you early and often. Make them sure that you always go above and beyond to serve them. I f you do not, then your product may quickly join the vast number of products that never really saw use.

Take a look at the App Store for your phone. How many of those products got downloaded once and never used again? Hook your customer from the start to build on the relationship with them instead of making them think you only wanted their money.

•Clean up messages and log entries

•Verify default values are correct and remove development values

•Test Install/Deployment on a new/clean machine

•Review the customer "unboxing" experience and common steps

•Avoid last minute changes, no matter how minor they may seem.

•Create and verify licensing, disclaimers, and other legal documentation

•Walk through getting started and user guides. Spot-checking is not enough

•Run all content possible through a spell-checker and look at grammar as well where possible.

•Verify consistent fonts, colors, and look-and-feel settings.

What are we thinking?

It is not uncommon for a software application to spend months or years in development and then be sunk by mistakes. Even worse, those errors could be fixed in minutes or hours. This begs the question of why such an obvious waste of all that development time occurs. The challenge is that there are a number of obstacles we face in our attempt to be thorough in our final steps of testing, deploying and packaging an application. Watch out for these pitfalls.

1. Deadlines have to be met. We all have goals and other deadlines that drive our product release cycles. That can make it easy to cut corners at the end while thinking the time saved has not real cost.

2. Just one more tweak. If you watch one of those baking/cooking shows you see the chef making touches to the platter up to the last second. We also try to do that with software. Unfortunately, it is way too easy for that little touch to introduce a major flaw or bug.

3. We tend to focus on the functionality that is being delivered. The user experience and other aspects that are not directly related to requirements fall into our blind spots. It is not intentional. We just get too used to cycling through the application and miss even big flaws like spelling or misaligned controls due to our blinders.

4. Lack of experience. These little problems can become monumental. However, we may not have experienced the cost of such mistakes in the past.

Slow And Steady Wins The Race

The common reasons for finishing errors can be reduced through intentional changes and processes. When we focus on getting the job done correctly. We can remove the worry about making our deadline. Then the risk of making errors due to pressure or feeling rushed plummets. The best way to do this is to adjust our deadlines and scope as needed to keep us away from that last minute dash.

This all goes back to proper planning, design, and estimation. The concepts we have hit on throughout this process are critical for us to finish strong. That alone should be reason enough for us to follow best practices from the beginning of our project all the way through the end and beyond.

The Bottom Line

We are getting to the end of our project at this point. There is a tendency to go heads down and plow heedlessly across the finish line. That needs to be avoided. When we stay the course and ensure that all of our tasks are completed fully it allows us to keep up the quality. We can add that last bit of polish that shows our customers how much we appreciate them.

Declaring Victory – Ship It!

The moment has come. All of that hard work has taken you to the end of the project. Now it is time to add those finishing touches and ship the solution to your users or customers. There are steps along the way that helped us work on deploying the solution but now we need to do it for real.

Although the final step of shipping your product or releasing it to users can be simple and informal, there are steps that should be taken to wrap it as a release. These guidelines will help you to avoid never-ending projects while providing ways for it to evolve even after you have released it "into the wild."

Packaging the Solution

We have all been on the receiving end of a software product before. This probably includes digital downloads we have installed as well as physical shrink-wrap products. Consider what those have, what you like, and what you wish was in the package. The bare minimum should be some instructions for installing the product. Applications may need user manuals and similar documentation as well.

An installation can be as simple as the click of a button. Often that is all it should be. Make sure you script or otherwise automate as much as possible. This process is the first interaction your customers have with the solution so make a good impression. Test your install as well as the solution. When you do so, make sure you have a "clean" machine to test the install. Many issues during installation come from forgetting a step or requirement.

Did You Forget Anything?

The packaging for your solution should be a one-stop-shop for everything a user or administrator needs. This includes your documentation and user guides. A good packaging experience will make it easy for someone to see where to proceed if they were given the deployment package and nothing else. In the package, use obvious names like "README", "Users Guide", "Install Instructions", and other names that leave no question about the contents. Likewise, ensure the files are in common formats such as RTF or PDF that do not require the customer to purchase another piece of software. The system requirements and associated expectations should be easy to find and often are best placed in the README file or an equivalent.

The Unboxing Experience

A physical product has the opportunity to have an unboxing experience as part of its appeal. I think Apple does this best although there are other products that are excellent in this area. A good start in evaluating your approach (and stealing ideas) is to Google "unboxing videos" or "unboxing stories." This is a quick way to get some good ideas from companies that have mastered the process. A search like this will show that even simple things can be packaged in a way that creates a memorable experience.

More On The Unboxing Experience

The good news is that digital products can create at least as impressive an experience as the physically packaged ones. You can attempt this effect during the installation, but a startup process or getting started tutorial are even better. The best examples of these highlight the strengths of the solution while walking the user through everything they need to get started. The best solutions are an excellent way to lead users through the registration process, configuring preferences, and even solving their problem for the first time. Thus, you can serve the dual-purpose of helping the user customize their system while also getting them comfortable with their new purchase and even reduce new-user support calls.

Never forget that referrals are an important part of the success of any product. A good unboxing or getting started process can help you master this form of marketing. Do not stop with getting customers to buy your product. Take the steps to get them to love it and tell their friends.

Features of Good Packaging

- **An easy installation process**, provide defaults where possible.
- **An un-install process**. Make it easy to clean up the system when the user is done with your product.
- **Easy registration**. Do not make it a headache to utilize the license or enter product keys.
- **User Guides and Tutorials**. These can be online to make for easy updates and corrections.
- **Clear Instructions** for how to reach you. Support should be easy to access.
- **Easy to understand** naming of files, folders, and scripts.
- **Test the install process** many times and many ways. It is critical that the install go smoothly.
- **A Thank –you.** Be polite and courteous to your customer. Thank them for their purchase.

About The Author

Rob Broadhead (rob@rb-sns.com) is a seasoned veteran of IT. His roles and jobs have ranged from lowly developer and small companies to CIO functions and multi-national corporations. Not necessarily at the same time. :) Rob enjoys building software in teams and always has small side projects he is working on as well. These products include commercial shrink-wrap applications, shareware products, digital only solutions and SAAS solutions among others.

He is passionate about sharing his experiences with others in an attempt to help them learn from his mistakes. This includes numerous blogs posts for his consulting company RB Consulting, Inc. (rb-sns.com) and the educational site Develpreneur.com. He is the host of the Develprenur: Building Better Developers podcast and a frequent presenter in the weekly mentoring sessions.

In his free time he enjoys playing ice hockey, a glass of wine, catching up on the latest NetFlix shows or hanging out with his five children.

Thank You! I hope your time spent reading this book is well-rewarded.

For more templates to help with building software, answers to your questions, or to help with your project, please contact us on the rb-sns.com site. (https://rb-sns.com/)